# The *Unique* Wood Duck

Tableau of a Field Trip with
Frank Bellrose and Scott Nielsen

by

## Richard E. McCabe

## A Wildlife Management Institute Book

## Published by STACKPOLE BOOKS

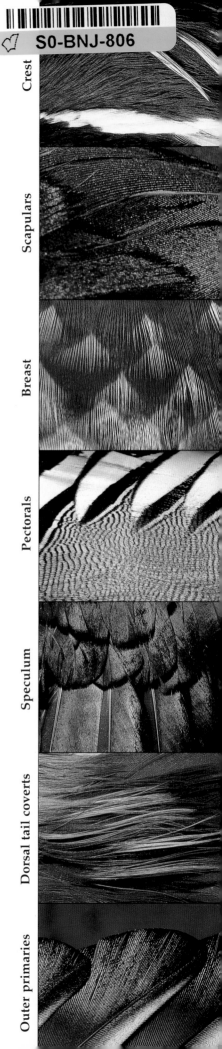

Crest

Scapulars

Breast

Pectorals

Speculum

Dorsal tail coverts

Outer primaries

The **Wildlife Management Institute (WMI)** is a private, nonprofit, scientific and educational organization founded in 1911. Based in Washington, D.C., WMI is dedicated to the restoration and wise use of North America's natural resources, especially wildlife, through professional management and cooperative public involvement. WMI's mission includes the preparation and dissemination of literature pertinent to public understanding, sound decision making and scientific management of wildlife resources. *The Unique Wood Duck* is one of more than 25 wildlife books produced by WMI. Other current WMI titles published by Stackpole Books are:

· *Ecology and Management of the Wood Duck*--Bellrose and Holm (1994)
· *Ecology and Management of the Mourning Dove*--Baskett, Tomlinson, Mirarchi, and Sayre, eds. (1993)
· *White-tailed Deer: Ecology and Management*--Halls, ed. (1984)
· *Elk of North America Ecology and Management*--Thomas and Toweill, eds. (1982)
· *Ducks, Geese and Swans of North America*--Bellrose (1981)
· *Big Game of North America: Ecology and Management*--Schmidt and Gilbert, eds. (1978)

For additional information about WMI's programs, publications and membership, write to: Wildlife Management Institute, 1101 14th Street, N.W., Suite 801, Washington, D.C. 20005.

THE UNIQUE WOOD DUCK
Copyright © 1993 by the Wildlife Management Institute
Published by Stackpole Books
    5067 Ritter Road
    Mechanicsburg, Pennsylvania 17055
Printed in Hong Kong

Library of Congress Cataloging-in-Publication Data

McCabe, Richard E.
    The unique wood duck : tableau of a field trip with Frank
Bellrose and Scott Nielsen / by Richard E. McCabe.
        p.   cm.
    "A Wildlife Management Institute book."
    ISBN 0-8117-3099-9
    1. Wood duck—North America.   2. Wood duck—North
America—Pictorial works.   I. Bellrose, Frank Chapman, 1916-
II. Nielsen, Scott.   III. Title.
    QL696.A52M38   1993                           92-46903
    598.4'1—dc20                                      CIP

**Book design and layout by Richard and Michael McCabe**

## PREFACE...

This publication was conceived as a companion volume to the important and superb book, *Ecology and Management of the Wood Duck*, by Frank Bellrose and Daniel Holm, produced by the Wildlife Management Institute and published by Stackpole Books. So extensive was the Bellrose-Holm benchmark work in its coverage of the wood duck life history, biology and management, and so impressive was its style and presentation—including hundreds of black and white photographs--that inclusion of color photos would have dramatically increased its cost and price. The inspiration for a separate, color book, as a complement to the "big book" on woodies, came from friend Mike Beno, former managing editor of *Ducks Unlimited* magazine.

I decided that the effort had to be something more than a pictorial essay or photo montage. It ought to be, like the wood duck itself, something unique. From that conviction came the idea to fashion this book as a field trip to the secret haunts of the wood duck. As guides, we enlisted the world's foremost authority on waterfowl and particularly wood ducks, Frank C. Bellrose, and unquestionably one of the world's best waterfowl photographers, Scott Nielsen. Who better to join on an informal field trip to witness the fascinating world of the woodie? Interestingly, Frank and Scott have never met in person, but they joined in the camaraderie of this publication adventure with eagerness and complete cooperation. They shared fully of their knowledge of the species through lengthy interviews, innumerable phone conversations and a two-year blizzard of correspondence. For their patient collaboration with me and infectious enthusiasm about the wood duck, I am extremely grateful.

But this book is not about Frank or Scott; it's about the woodie, *Aix sponsa*, a North American waterfowl species so unique and elegant that it seems somehow to transcend the intricate and sometimes perplexing labyrinth of biology. It seems, more so, to be living art, in the form and substance of a duck.

Most of the photographs featured on the pages to follow were taken by Scott Nielsen. Other contributors are identified alongside their scenes. I wish to extend special thanks for assistance on this publication to Keith Harmon for editorial review, Kelly Glidden for manuscript coordination, and my son Mike McCabe, who was instrumental in the book's layout.

This work is dedicated to North America's waterfowl biologists—as energetic, dedicated and often beleaguered a cadre of professionals as I have known and with whom I have had opportunity to associate.

Richard E. McCabe

## FRANK BELLROSE...

I can't rightfully say that the wood duck is my favorite waterfowl species, even though it is the one I have been privileged to study most closely for more than 50 years. I can't even agree entirely with those who think the woodie is the most beautiful of North American ducks. If truth be told, I have no favorites among the waterfowl species. But perhaps more accurately, they are all favorites. And I honestly see as much beauty in one species as the next. Each is distinctive and holds separate fascinations. Certainly the most colorful duck--the wood duck--is special because, in my opinion at least, it is the most unique.

But not even the woodie's uniqueness is what triggered my initial interest in it or what prompted my studies of it or has sustained my enthusiasm for the species. My careerlong investigations into the amazing world of the wood duck have been largely a result of coincidence.

I'm afraid that some people give me more credit for intelligence and foresight than really is the case. I'm actually pretty average in those regards. But I do admit to great curiosity. I suppose that's an attribute. At the very least, it is convenient compensation.

Curiosity, along with a liberal amount of luck, has proven a good combination for me. I was lucky, for example, to have been born and raised along the Illinois River in westcentral Illinois and in a family that not only condoned but encouraged my intrigues, and certainly those about the outdoors. I also was fortunate to have discovered the writings and teachings of such mentors as Aldo Leopold, the "father" of modern wildlife management, Benjamin T. Gault, a pioneering ornithologist, Bob Becker, outdoor editor of *The Chicago Tribune*, and eventually to have made their acquaintance. I was especially lucky to have had parents who were willing to sacrifice a great deal during the Depression years to enable me to get a college education. I feel lucky to have been hired by the Illinois Natural History Survey in the late '30s and to have been paired at the outset with a fellow waterfowl biologist, Art Hawkins. It was especially fortuitous to have been professionally located within the Illinois River Valley, which had then and still has a large population of nesting wood ducks. And I feel especially fortunate to have been allowed to maintain my home and research base in Havana. This was due in very large measure to the support of my bosses over the years, including Theodore Frison, Harlow Mills, Tom Scott and Glen Sanderson.

It has been my luck as well to have been surrounded by or otherwise associated with people of considerable enthusiasm, remarkable dedication and similar inquisitiveness. Not least of all, I consider myself lucky indeed to have a wife and sons who have always been encouraging of my work.

My first exposure to ornithology was back in 1929. A Boy Scout then, I was bent on qualifying for as many merit badges as possible. Peer competition was a strong motivation, and one such merit badge called for identifying 40 species of birds. I thought the requirement insurmountable and told my father that I didn't think there were 40 different birds in the vicinity of our home in Ottawa. My father armed me with a bird book and field glasses and urged me to find out. It wasn't long before the locating and identifying of birds became a serious interest. It persisted long after the merit badge was secured and my fellow Scouts turned their attentions elsewhere.

Like many youngsters of the time, I was enthralled with stories of outdoor adventure. *Boy's Life* and books by Burroughs and others were avidly read. At age 10, I started hiking the fields and woodlots outside Ottawa and at my grandmother's farm on the Fox River at Bellrose Dells near Wedron. I first camped there when I was 11, and for a number of summers afterward, I camped there for a month or two. My father taught me how to trap and fish and otherwise gain familiarity with the natural environment. In high school, I organized a Junior Audubon Club. It all seemed and probably was pretty normal. In any case, those experiences gave opportunity and vent for a growing curiosity about the natural world.

*Mike Beno*

In 1930, when I was 14, my parents bought me a canoe, and I found that paddling that area's waterways was not only a great release for adolescent energies but also allowed me to visit a theretofore hidden world of mystery on and along the area's streams. With friends, I would set out and paddle the quiet waters or sloughs for as far as my father could drive to pick me up at a predetermined time and place.

The sights, sounds and smells of those water courses were perfect fuel for a boy's questioning nature and yen for "wilderness" adventure. The world visited by canoe is a very special place.

Early in the '30s, the Illinois River was dammed below Ottawa. The resulting impoundment flooded a lot of agricultural land, and it wasn't long before there appeared a wide variety of duck species not previously frequent to the area. The impoundment and its backwaters always seemed to hold ducks, and it was easy for me to ride my bike there and observe them. My ornithological fascination shifted then from songbirds to waterfowl.

As I recall, my first sighting of wood ducks was when I was canoeing a slough above the Starved Rock dam on the Illinois River. In a slow and sheltered stretch of the river, I witnessed a number of wood ducks in eclipse plumage. They were swimming back and forth among clusters of cattails. That was about the time I graduated from high school in 1934.

At college, I studied ornithology. When asked about employment or a career, I told people that I wanted to study waterfowl. That was a response that most either didn't understand or believe. And as supportive as my parents were, they too had doubts, informing me that duck study might be a good hobby, but it very likely was not something someone could do for a living. The closer I was to graduation, and with jobs of any sort at a premium, the less sure I was too.

As I saw it then, my recourses to "duck study" were few indeed. In fact, my only hope seemed to lie in going for an advanced degree at an out-of-state university.

The dilemma was short-lived. At precisely that time, the Illinois Natural History Survey--which was just starting a wildlife research section--was looking to employ someone to study waterfowl. I applied and, by great good fortune, was hired to study waterfowl at the confluence of the Illinois and Mississippi rivers--an area soon thereafter to be partly flooded by the Alton Navigation Dam. I was paired with Art Hawkins and stationed at Brussels, Illinois. It was long after my duties began when Milford Smith, an employee at the newly established Chatauqua National Wildlife Refuge, showed me a number of natural cavities used by nesting wood ducks. I suggested to Art that we relocate our base of operation from Brussels to Havana, and this was accomplished. That was in 1938. The Survey Chief then, Dr. Frison, advised us that he expected us to return to Brussels when the area flooded. It never happened. Instead, the Survey established a laboratory on the Chatauqua Refuge.

Since those early days, and thanks to a great many people, I have been able to concentrate my energies on waterfowl--not just wood ducks, but all kinds, and particularly the puddlers. If nothing else, my career has proven that someone really can make a living doing what they enjoy most--even studying ducks.

The wood duck, though, as I previously noted, is special to me. It is special because it was where I was able to investigate it closely, which was a definite advantage. And its habitat preference, physiology and behaviors have convinced me over the span of a half century that it truly is the most unique of North American waterfowl. To be sure, I am biased in this regard, but the data clearly support that view.

One does not need to see data to discover the wood duck's uniqueness. One merely has to have even slight opportunity to observe these birds in the wild. And such opportunity has been mine, by coincidence, luck and choice.

*SCOTT NIELSEN...*

Our world is full of people who look but don't necessarily see; people who know a lot but often understand little. For me, the change began early in March 1974, when an accumulated winter's snowfall caved in the roof of my garage in northwestern Wisconsin. Most of the erstwhile garage ended up as scrap lumber and kindling. But on a whim, I also used some of the splintered planks to fashion a wood duck nest house. It was placed in a balsam tree along the lakeshore less than 70 feet from my home.

I made every mistake possible in construction of the nest house and in its siting. Fortunately, an equally inexperienced hen wood duck showed up a month later and set up housekeeping. Each succeeding year brought new houses and more ducks until, in 1979, seven hens were choosing between 20 nest houses.

Earlier that year, I had been invited to write an article for *Ducks Unlimited* on taxidermy--my main vocation at that time. In the process of drafting the piece for DU's magazine, I purchased and taught myself how to use the photography equipment necessary to take pictures to accompany the article. It seemed ridiculous to let such expensive "toys" lay idle after the article's completion, so I combined my two growing interests and spent that spring trying to "capture" my feathered tenants on film.

Much as with my first wood duck house, I made every mistake imaginable during that 1979 season, and the resulting photos proved it. But I was more than compensated by the experiences I had with the birds--experiences that I never would have had the time, effort and incentive to seek out otherwise.

A trend was started and has continued since--with better nest houses, more hens and fancier photo gear each year. Nevertheless, my underlying reasons for photographing woodies remain the same. The experience and enjoyment I receive from "my" ducks are just as relaxing, novel, exciting and fulfilling today as they were when I shuttered my first picture in '79. The photographs have gotten technically better, but that's merely the proverbial frosting on the cake. Photography is just a tool rather than an end in itself; it is an excuse for me to go out, work with the birds and see what they can teach me about the world I share with them.

The photos in this book are not just images of a magnificent waterfowl species; they are a sampling of my experiences with those birds. I hope, as with all my photographs, that viewers will look at them from several standpoints--biological, ecological and aesthetic. Note, for example, how beautiful the wood duck is in all its elements--air, land and water. On closer examination, see how perfectly adapted these birds are to their unique niche in the natural world. As a taxidermist, I have dissected and reassembled dozens of wood ducks, learning every feather and muscle in the process. As a photographer, I learned how every anatomical aspect of the woodie fits neatly and importantly to form a unified whole. Yet, the wood duck is, indeed, much more than the sum of its parts. I continue to marvel at how regal this bird is-- not only its brilliant coloration, but also how exceptionally functional and adaptive the wood duck is to its natural environment. *That* is the relationship I try to show with my photos.

In addition, I like to photograph the wood duck as an interactive bird. Woodies move within a society that, in many ways, is as interesting as our own, yet they do so with more subtlety, simplicity and grace. I usually am much more comfortable, intrigued and alert in the company of a flock of wood ducks than I am with a group of people. I hope some of the senses of tranquility and joy that woodies radiate and evoke are evident in the photos.

Realize, too, what a small portion of their life is being shown. At an average shutter speed of 1/60 of a second per photo, this collection represents less than three seconds in a few of their lives. Extend that to a realistic woodie lifetime of a year or two or more, and multiply that result by more than a million other individual wood ducks and you have an inkling of the large contribution this species makes to the natural fabric and intrinsic value of our world.

Economists are fond of putting a dollar and cents value on everything, including our natural heritage. But to me, the wood duck is not a commodity to be appraised, assessed or distinguished by pecuniary standards of any kind. Instead, the woodie is a living symbol of the integrity and vitality of a whittled-down natural world, and that symbolism can't be measured in any monetary terms I know or want to know. I hope that my photographs are reminders that wood ducks contribute to their own habitats *and* to ours, and that those sur-roundings, however fragile, are one and the same.

*Mary Ann Grymala*

As with all art mediums, photography is a translation. And as with all translations, something inevitably is lost or missed in the artistic process. Photography, by virtue of its technology, is a subtractive art form. When I press the shutter, judgments already have been made about the scene or perspective that I want to capture, what portion of the overall setting I wish to frame in the photograph, how to balance image clarity and subject distance, and which millisecond of drama is to be visually preserved on film. Each judgment involves a conscious deletion of certain actions and features. Each set of judgments that trigger the shutter just once is a distancing from reality--an emphasis on the moment rather than on the continuum of time itself. As I view every new photo, I tend to be more critical of what was omitted from the scene than of what was captured in fractional time and place.

My hope is that this volume encourages readers to make and take time to get out in nature and, above all, to experience it. Wood ducks are a wonderful catalyst, but the list of subjects is endless. And the tools besides photography that can be used for that adventure and enjoyment and their translation are almost as infinite. My investments of a few dozen nest houses, a few hundred rolls of film and a few thousand hours of time, in turn have given me enduring experiences and pleasure for which no amount of money or recognition could compensate or substitute.

I think back to early April mornings when the first small flocks of woodies set into the snow-lined creek behind my house. I reflect on the pairs and trios that glide effortlessly around the lake's open margins a week later, seeking out food and housing. I reminisce about the dramas of courtship and mating that follow, and recall the sight of wood ducks at sunrise, ornamentally perched in trees just outside my livingroom window. I remember, too, the quiet of early May, when drakes desert their mates, and the hens in turn spend most of their days in the silent maternal solitude of nest houses. And I am reminded of that silence finally broken on a late May morning when a hen calls a new generation down from its birthplace and into a new world.

These things I remember just as vividly as if they had happened yesterday, and I look forward to many more seasons with the wood duck, with ever-better focus. My interest in nature has widened considerably since that first homely nest house. But no matter where things lead me, I always come back to the wood duck, because that's where, for me, a new perspective, a new enthusiasm and a new art form began. Through the wood duck, I began to see and understand what a spectacular world it is that we share with them.

Others can have much the same experiences, whether with ducks, deer, daisies, Douglas-fir, dogfish, dragonflies, dandelions or daddy longlegs. It's easy, fun and infinitely rewarding.

More than anything, I hope this work serves not as a substitute for experiences, but rather as a starting point for readers' broader and better personal relationship with nature. For certain, it is a cheaper beginning than having one's garage roof collapse.

*Frank...* The woodie was first introduced to the world as the "Summer Duck," as called by John Catesby. That common name apparently was given because the species was by far the most prevalent waterfowl during summer months in the Southeast where Catesby made his observations in the early 1700s. "Wood duck" seems to have emerged as a colloquialism--and was widely accepted by the mid-1800s--with reference to the species preference for forested habitats. Over the years, the woodie has been the recipient of at least 22 other common names, including Carolina duck, Carolina teal, bridal duck, squealer, regal duck, rainbow duck, plumer and black-billed whistling duck.

In North America, only four duck species are the sole representative of their genus--the wood duck (*Aix*), Stellar's eider (*Polysticta*), harlequin duck (*Histrionicus*) and oldsquaw (*Clangula*). Worldwide, the woodie shares its genus only with the mandarin duck (*Aix galericulata*) of Asia.

*Scott...* From strictly a beauty standpoint, I would separate the world's duck species into size categories. Among the small ducks, the Baikal teal is especially attractive. Of the mid-sized ducks, the mandarin and wood duck are decidedly beautiful. The king eider certainly is a particularly striking large duck. But beauty in ducks, as in most things, is a composite impression. To me, no duck lacks appeal.

The mandarin and woodie are products of millions of years of refined evolution. Both are survivors eminently adapted and suited to their separate roles in their separate environments. That makes them equally beautiful to me.

*Frank...* Wood duck and mandarin drakes share similar colored side feathers, crested head and white belly. The vermiculated sides of the wood duck are separated from the burgundy by a vertical black and white bar; in the mandarin, there are two black and two white vertical stripes. Most notable of the mandarin drake is its sail-like *outermost* secondary, unusual among all waterfowl. The sail is analogous to the outer tertial feather of the wood duck drake.

Wood duck and mandarin females are very similar except for the white markings behind the eyes--it is teardrop shaped in the wood duck and a narrow stripe in the mandarin.

The mandarin breeds in eastern China and in Siberia largely north of the Korean peninsula. It winters in Japan, southern China and Formosa.

Mandarins are slightly smaller than wood ducks; the males are 20 percent smaller, and the females 25 percent. Although the eyes of mandarins are smaller than the exceptionally large eyes of the wood ducks, they are proportionately slightly larger than the woodies'.

*Scott...* Mandarin ducks and woodies are what ornithologists term "ecological replacements." That is, the mandarin in Asia occupies similar habitat and has a niche within that habitat as does the wood duck in North America.

Where the species are placed together in captivity, hybridization is rare. The reason may be due in part to the fact that the hens of both species select their mates, not vice versa. And the obvious differences among drakes of the two species allow the hens to discriminate easily in favor of their own kind. Also, it has been established that the two species have different numbers of chromosomes, making successful interbreeding nearly impossible.

*Frank...* The pre-Columbian abundance of wood ducks is uncertain, but the species was well-known to North America's native peoples prehistorically, particularly in the Southeast and Mississippi River Valley regions. Archeological and ethnological research has revealed that woodies were represented in the ceremonies, crafts and effigies of some Indian groups or cultures at least as early as 100 A.D.

Woodies are medium-sized ducks, smaller than mallard and larger than teal. Adult males average 1.5 pounds; females and juveniles weigh only slightly less. By contrast, adult drake mallards weigh 2.8 pounds and adult blue-winged teal weigh 1.0 pound. And because of its large tail, the wood duck, at 20 inches in length, is nearly equidistant between the lengths of a mallard (25 inches) and a blue-winged teal (16 inches). Another cavity-nesting species, the hooded merganser approaches the overall dimensions of the woodie more than any other species does.

*Scott...* Most guidebooks and other references about waterfowl make note of the hen wood duck's "drab" coloration. That is true only in contrast to her brilliantly colored mate. In most every other comparison, the woodie hen has great but subtle beauty, including delicate patterns of gray shading and quite a fair amount of iridescence. She has a crest only slightly less prominent than the drake's, though hers is on display relatively infrequently.

The female plumage is as well-suited to its gender roles as the male's is to its. The egg-laying and brooding hen needs colors and markings that help shield her from the view of predators. This is especially necessary during her coming and going from the nest cavity and for the subsequent two months while she escorts her ducklings until they are capable of flight.

Drake wood ducks use their colorful plumage to attract the attention of hens seeking prospective mates.

*Frank...* The wood duck has the largest eyes of any duck species in North America. Although large eyes would seem to enable birds to see better in twilight, other waterfowl--such as Canada geese and teal--are active at dusk, as is the wood duck.  The great blue heron feeds when it is quite dark, yet it has smaller eyes.  Even the nocturnal black-crowned night-heron has smaller eyes than does the woodie.  Therefore, I believe more is involved with the wood duck's eye size than light intensity.  They probably are so large to enable woodies to see peripheral objects so necessary when these ducks fly among the canopy of trees that are the species' usual haunts.

The drake's red eyes must be part of a sexual adornment, even though that color highlight seems superfluous.  Male canvasbacks and  common and red-breasted mergansers  also have red irises, as do Arctic, common and red-throated loons, western, horned and eared grebes, adult and immature yellow-crowned night-herons, adult black-crowned, white-faced glossy ibises, and probably limpkins.

**Scott...** The position of the wood duck's eyes on the side of its head allows an exceptionally wide field of vision. This is important not only for flight among trees, but also as an early warning system necessary for a bird that spends most of its time on water or land where a full range of predators can approach closely.

Complementing the woodie's exceptional eyesight is a very acute sense of hearing. Danger in forested bottomlands frequently is heard before it is seen. Evidence indicates that the wood duck may have a better sense of smell than do other waterfowl species.

**Frank...** The wood duck's bill is shorter and narrower than that of most other dabbling ducks. The hooked end enables them to peck and tear at edible vegetation, such as tubers and the matrix of lotus heads, to extract seeds or fruit.

Woodies also are able to grasp fish, frogs and small insects in their bills. I have watched adult wood ducks leap off water to snare insects off trees and shrub leaves and branches. And it is not uncommon for woodie ducklings to jump up to catch low-flying insects. They are successful in these attempts a majority of the time.

The wood duck's narrow tongue serves in part to align foods properly before swallowing. Acorns, for example, always are swallowed with the pointed end down. Consumed otherwise, the sharp mast tip could seriously damage the duck's esophagus.

**Scott...** The wood duck's bill is highly adapted for grasping and plucking preferred food, such as mast. Its particular fondness for acorns earned it the sobriquet "acorn duck" in early days. Other dabbling ducks, such as the black duck, have relatively longer and spoonlike bills more exclusively adapted for sifting through watery vegetation.

Wood ducks occasionally compete with hooded mergansers, a diving duck, for nesting cavities, but they have dissimilar food habitats and feeding habits. Mergansers' long, narrow bills are suited to catching small fish and aquatic invertebrates rather than dabbling (puddling) the surface of water for floating plant and animal foods.

*Frank...* For all its brilliant plumage, the male wood duck is amazingly camouflaged in its wooded habitats. Its many-angled "flowing" white lines break its head and body shapes into fairly indistinct bits and pieces. The light and shadow of surrounding vegetation further diffuses any solid shape.

I often have observed male wood ducks resting prone on a "driftwood gray" log. Surprisingly, their bronze side feathers blend imperceptibly into the log's hue.

The somber brown-gray plumage of the female blends into the shadowy background of overhead woody cover to which they retreat after sunrise, reappearing into the open only before sunset or on dark cloudy days. The white-flecked chests and breasts and white throats of both males and females break head-on views of that part of the body into segments that lack clear conformation.

The lighter lower parts of the body of both drakes and hens--being in greater shadow--appear dark and, therefore, do not appear distinct from the dark backs, particularly when the woodies are perched in trees.

*Scott...* The hens of most duck species are shades of brown, to blend in with the grasses and other vegetation in which they commonly nest. The hen wood duck's grayish overall color is better suited to dying or dead weathered trees and snags in which it finds nest cavities. Both drake and hen woodies are surprisingly well-camouflaged when in their forested habitats. People may be used to seeing these birds in zoos and other aviaries where the drake's brilliant colors are in gaudy contrast to the artificial enclosures. But in natural cover, the bold colors and patterns are broken up. Even with my telephoto lens, I often have difficulty locating them.

***Frank...*** Once, from the vantage of a 100-foot tower, I watched males and pairs of wood ducks swimming and feeding 150 feet or more from flooded woody cover at daybreak. As the light intensity increased, they slowly maneuvered toward a wooded shoreline. Even though I was looking down at a 20-degree angle, the ducks disappeared from sight as soon as a few wooded branches broke up their plumage pattern. I am constantly amazed at the "disappearing" effect of slight overhead cover on their visibility.

***Scott...*** Many species of wildlife have lighter undersides than backs, a principle biologists term "countershading." In this way, a predator viewing the individual from below would see a light belly blending in with an equally light sky or water surface. From above, the individual's dark backside would blend with the similarly dark earth tones. That's the theory, but there are many exceptions to the rule, such as the black duck and shoveler among dabbling ducks.

*Frank...* Wood ducks are committed to riverine habitat more so than is any other duck species, but they also occupy a wide assortment of wetlands, including swamps, overflow bottomland flats, marshes, beaver ponds and farm ponds.

As a result of their necessity to nest in trees--to avoid nest inundation on the ground and ground predators--woodies have evolved an ability to perch in trees, unlike any other North American duck.  They often perch on branches as small as a finger because of the dexterity of their elongated toes to bend and lock on a small surface. Whistling ducks and muscovies also perch in trees, but most of these are in the southern hemisphere.

*Scott...* Wood ducks perch much more frequently than other North American ducks, including other dabbling ducks, partly because of their selection of forested habitats and their anatomical adaptation to elevated locations out of the reach of most predators.

The woodie's toenails are longer and more curved than other ducks', and their legs are more forward of the body than most other waterfowl. These characteristics enable them to maintain a relaxed horizontal position, yet a firm grasp, while perched.

Diving ducks, with legs located closer to the tail to facilitate relatively better propulsion when swimming underwater and on rough open water, perch less commonly than do dabbling ducks generally and the wood duck especially. To perch, most divers must remain somewhat awkwardly erect in order to place their center of gravity over their legs and feet.

For elevated perches, wood ducks seem to have strong preference for shoreline trees with limbs and branches extending over water.

*Frank...* Mallards can perch on logs, stumps and other broad surfaces, but do not have the proficiency with their feet to grasp small surfaces. Diving ducks, such as the ring-neck, have even less nimbleness and flexibility in their toes.

*Stephen Kirkpatrick*

*Scott...* Most birds, including waterfowl, rest on one leg from time to time. This probably is done to rest one leg yet maintain dry airflow underneath the body. I see one-legged stances most often in the cooler months, so the posture may enable the bird to warm the withdrawn leg and foot. The woodie's legs and feet, as with other ducks, have low blood circulation so can endure extreme cold. But unless warmed periodically, they could be frozen.

*Frank...* Next to the mallard, the wood duck has the most extensive diet of any duck. For most of the year, the diet is based on carbohydrates--acorns, pecans, other mast, corn, rice, wheat, smartweeds, millets and other weed seeds. However, during prelaying and laying, hens turn to invertebrates to obtain protein needed in egg formation. Early developing ducklings also require a high protein diet necessary for rapid growth. They change from invertebrates to high plant protein (such as duckweeds) when about a month old.

The wood duck searches for food four ways: pecking at objects on the surface of the water; tipping up to reach items in shallow water; walking through groves of oak trees, pecan and philbert orchards, and harvested corn and wheat fields searching for nuts and grains; and diving for acorns and corn in shallow water.

Acorns are their basic food from early autumn through winter, especially in the South where several species of oaks grow in bottomlands subject to flooding. Wood ducks utilize acorns more than does any other duck species.

*Stephen Kirkpatrick*

*Scott...* Woodies frequently tip up to reach submerged food less than a foot below the waterline.

Wood ducks occasionally will dive to retrieve a favorite food item, such as acorns. Their strength in relation to other dabbling ducks enables them to go to depths of three or four feet and remain underwater for four to eight seconds. This is in contrast to heavier bodied diving ducks that can dive to 10 to 20 foot depths and remain submerged for 30 seconds or more.

When woodies dive, it usually is because they have observed food below the surface. It's rare that they dive to forage.

*Frank...* I once saw a captive wood duck swim underwater several times around a plastic wading pool. The duck used its wings as well as its legs and feet to propel itself with surprising speed.

Wood ducks dive by lurching forward out of the water in a tight arc. The higher the arc, the deeper the dive. The feet and legs thrust forward to provide the momentum. The streamlined head enters the water first, and the wings are compressed against the body to minimize resistance.

*Scott...* I have seen wood ducks dive to escape birds of prey or escape detection by predators. They use their webbed feet in unison to propel themselves several yards to or in the direction of shelter.

When woodies are diving for food in pairs or trios, they seem to take turns diving. One duck invariably is on the surface when its companion(s) is underwater. Presumably, the surfaced bird is a lookout for danger. I have witnessed this consistent behavior so often that it can't be coincidence.

*Frank...* Although diving is not a common feeding behavior, woodies do so more than any other dabbling duck. It also dabbles on the surface more than any other dabbler or diver. And when competing for waste corn in harvested fields, wood ducks can outrun any other duck.

On water, woodies swim as fast as most other ducks, including such divers as the canvasback.

*Scott...* Wood ducks use flight to escape danger, move
to feeding, loafing and roosting areas, migrate in
response to daylight length and food supply,
locate and compete for mates, and reach elevated
cavities for nesting.

*Frank...* In proportion to its size, the wood duck
has the broadest wing of any game duck.
Its wing width, along with its broad tail,
may have evolved to facilitate flight
among the branches of trees.

*Scott...* The long and slender wings of such species as the canvasback, ring-necked duck and pintail are adapted to rapid flight in open areas where sudden changes of direction aren't often necessary. By virtue of its wing shape, the woodie sacrifices speed in favor of maneuverability.

Large breast (pectoral) muscles and wings that are large in relation to its body weight enable wood ducks to leap quickly into vertical flight, whether off water, the ground or from perches. These characteristics also allow the flying wood duck to bank quickly side to side.

*Frank...* With relatively narrow and
shorter wings and legs positioned
farther back along their torsos,
diving ducks such as the ringneck
require a running start into the wind
to gain momentum for flight.

Wood ducks spring into the
air using their feet and legs to thrust
upward in concert with a powerful
initial downstroke of the wings.
Unlike mallards that commonly
"tower up" 40 to 60 feet from
flooded bottomland forest, wood
ducks--though capable of such
vertical ascensions--usually take off
at a 45-degree angle through wood-
land canopies.

*Scott...* The efficient mechanics of woodie take-off include a push of the feet against the water and a thrust of the head forward. The tail and raised wings "slap" downward. The woodie can "flush"from water and achieve elevation faster than other ducks. Sudden flight can produce a virtual explosion of water.

*Frank...* Unlike other ducks, such as the mallard, woodies rarely strike their wings on the water surface when taking flight.

In propelling upward or forward, the down stroke of the wood duck's wings is initially rotated forward and then downward. The 10 "flight" feathers (primaries) provide the forward thrust and the next 10 wing feathers (secondaries) are more for lift. The remaining three feathers (tertials) close to the body also provide lift.

A single wingstroke at take-off encompasses almost 170 degrees. In direct flight, wing motion covers about 120 degrees.

*Scott...* When a male and female wood duck are paired, the hen usually initiates the flight. And unless the pair is spooked by sudden danger, the drake is quick to follow its mate.

*Scott...* The wood duck's flight profile is quite distinctive. Even with the crests of both hens and drakes laid back to reduce drag, they give woodies the appearance of having an elongated and "blockie" head. The long, broad tail also is a give-away feature. And because of their large wings in relation to body mass, the wingbeats cause wood ducks to "bob" much more in flight than do other ducks.

Closest to the woodie in flight profile is the hooded merganser. But this diving duck has proportionately smaller wings and faster wing beats, so shows less undulating motion.

*Frank...* About one-third of all wood ducks breed where they winter. The others migrate 100 to 1,000 miles or so to return to previous nesting or natal areas. By waterfowl standards, such migratory distance is quite short.

By the time most woodies have begun their northward migration in February, some already have started nesting in the Deep South. Between the vanguards and laggards, the flight north may be spread over a period of six weeks. Direct band recoveries by latitude show that wood ducks spend little time between wintering and breeding areas. Most wood ducks venturing to the species' more northerly breeding areas have arrived there by May. Some may delay departure to the breeding areas if food supplies in the wintering area are plentiful and permit lipid (fat) storage. Spring migration flock size is about 10 wood ducks, but many arrive as pairs or trios.

*Scott...* Most migrational flights by wood ducks are at night. It seems that they wait for a favorable wind just before sunset.

*Frank...* The period of autumn migration by woodies spans about three months, depending mostly on weather and hunting pressure, with departures starting in early September and continuing to freeze-up of shallow waters, usually in November or December. Flock size during autumn migration is about 23.

*Frank...* Under any circumstance, prolonged flight--such as during migration--is a rapid drain on a wood duck's energy reserve. A flight of 500 miles under normal circumstances utilizes about 34 grams of fat, or roughly 5 percent of the adult woodie's body weight. Most wood ducks fly directly from breeding to wintering areas, with very few stops in between for any length of time.

The wood duck's flight speed averages 32 miles per hour, but wind-aided, may reach 37 miles per hour, which is slow compared with that of most other ducks. From the standpoint of energy conservation, the woodie's optimal flight speed in migration is 33 miles per hour.

*Scott...* Wood ducks spend a portion of each day--sometimes for as long as five hours straight--resting or loafing.  This usually occurs from midmorning to late afternoon.  A certain amount of movement is necessary, of course, for feeding, courtship, preening, nest site selection and building, etc., but resting is especially important for conserving energy.

***Frank...*** For female wood ducks, energy demands are greatest during the prelaying and egg laying periods, and during incubation, molt and migration.  For the drakes, energy is most rapidly expended in defending his mate against rival males and during molt and migration.

Because woodies migrate shorter distances than do other ducks, their energy requirements are less.

During winter months, wood ducks increase their consumption of foods high in carbohydrates, including acorns, pecans, corn and weed seeds, to help maintain their body temperatures at 101 to 105 degrees Fahrenheit (depending on activity).  Carbohydrates--from seeds--also are especially important to incubating hens in spring.

*Scott...* Resting or loafing during the day by wood ducks not only conserves energy but it reduces the birds' exposure to predators. A motionless wood duck is less easily detected than an active one.

As with any animal, including humans, comfort movements occasionally are needed to relieve or loosen tight or cramped inert muscles. Woodies infrequently stretch during rests and almost always after resting and before becoming active.

Yawning expels carbon dioxide built up in the respiratory system as a result of relatively shallow breathing during periods of rest and sleep.

*Think...* Wood duck habitats vary seasonally. They may be separated conveniently into several categories--breeding, postnuptial and wintering. Spring habitats would be a part of breeding habitat, and the habitats of autumn migration might be divided between postnuptial and wintering habitats.

*Breeding.* Wood ducks frequent most of the riverine habitats east of the Great Plains, and in scattered locations in riparian areas of the Great Plains. In addition, they utilize swamps, overflow bottomlands, beaver ponds, lakes and marshes. The quality of the food base, in conjunction with nest sites and the availability of desirable cover, determines the value of an area for wood ducks.

The lower the stream banks, the clearer the water and the greater the abundance of oxbows, cut-off channels and islands, the better the stream for breeding wood ducks.

*Postnuptial.* Food and cover needed during molting result in large numbers of wood ducks shifting to more marshlike areas. To do so, woodies may move hundreds of miles, especially to the north or west. These wetlands ideally have shallow water-- usually less than four feet--with beds of bulrushes, cattails, duck potatoes, arrowarum, pickerelweed, waterlilies, American lotus and similar aquatic plants.

During autumn, wood ducks seek flooded beds of maturing moist-soil plants, such as duck millet, smartweeds, nutgrasses and pigweed. They commonly fly one to five miles daily to feed on waste wheat or corn left in harvested fields, fallen nuts in orchards, or acorns in oak groves.

*Winter.* Wood ducks especially seek any overflow floodplains where rising water makes mast--acorns, pecans, seeds of buttonbush and swamp privet, etc.--available in shallow water. Where groves of oaks minimize understory vegetation, woodies feed on dry ground, seeking acorns and other mast. Where natural foods are lacking, they utilize waste corn and rice in fields.

I believe that the optimal habitats for woodies, except during winter, are found in the Upper Mississippi River Valley. The region's wooded sloughs and marshes are ideal because of the exceptional interspersion and juxtaposition of water, timber and marsh.

*Scott...* Wood ducks bathe once or twice a day to remove, loosen or dissolve insects, soil and any other debris that accumulates in their feathers. Bathing often occurs after feeding; a woodie may have spent an hour or two previously in that vicinity without experiencing disturbance, so feels reasonably safe in dousing itself with water for less than a minute before flapping, shaking, preening and sunning away the water. Movements during bathing are quick and vigorous.

A waterproof bird such as the wood duck expends a fair amount of energy working the water into its feathers. It facilitates this by separating or fluffing up its feathers so that water can flow in between them.

*Frank...* Bathing serves two purposes--as part of the courtship ritual by both sexes, and to help rid the plumage of dirt, ectoparasites (such as feather lice), stale preen oil, bits of skin, feather particles, etc.

Bathing is especially evident in the hen following copulation. Males bathe more rarely as part of their postcopulatory displays.

*Scott...* Bathing intensity by wood ducks varies. A light or partial bath, followed by wing flapping, occurs more often than the once or twice daily thorough bath. The thorough bath necessitates more seclusion or safer surroundings, since drying and preening can take an hour or more. Feathers must be dry and in place for maximum flight (escape) capability.

During bathing, wood ducks commonly dip or dunk their heads. Because the woodie's feathers are heavily waterproofed, vigorous and repeated motion is needed for water to penetrate. Despite each dousing motion, much more water runs off or beads up than actually cleanses.

*Frank...* Wing flapping serves two purposes for wood ducks. First, it sheds water from flight feathers at the conclusion of bathing and periodically during feeding by tipping-up or diving in water and during periods of precipitation. Second, it provides a release of tension during sexual encounters.

*Scott...* Wet wings are a liability to the wood duck, as well as any other bird that uses flight to escape danger.

Whenever water accumulates on the wings, most commonly after bathing, a woodie will push its body forward and upward by arching its back, lifting its tail and treading vigorously. In this erect posture, the wings are outstretched and flapped intensely several times. Depending on the degree of dampness and particularly after bouts of diving, this flapping may be repeated several times. Wing flapping almost always is followed right away by preening.

*Frank...* Bathing is an important aspect of the courtship sequence. And since wing flapping invariably follows bathing-- especially by hens--it too must be considered part of the mating ritual.

*Scott...* Preening is the most important thing wood ducks and
other birds do to maintain the
structure and vitality of their
feathers, which are essential for
flight, insulation and waterproofing.

*Frank...* Preening benefits wood
ducks in a number of significant ways.  It repairs feather
structure, adds oil to enhance
waterproofing, rids plumage of
dirt, stale preen oil, ectoparasites and other exudates, and
aids in removal of small feathers during molt.

*Scott...* Woodies, like other ducks, spend quite a lot of time preening their thousands of feathers. If feathers are soiled or out of order, wood ducks will immediately groom themselves. Once or twice a day, they will spend an hour or more preening from head to tail. One session usually is midmorning, after feeding and bathing.

Once a wood duck bathes, flaps its wings and shakes to remove excess water, it will retire to a quiet, safe, often elevated spot or perch to preen. Preening sometimes is done in dense cover, but woodies seem to prefer sunny openings in trees or on water where they can have a reasonable view of approaching predators and where sunlight can help in drying.

The wood duck uses its bill to do most preening, grasping each feather to smooth and arrange it so that its parts lock together properly (much like velcro). Flight feathers usually are given first attention,

*Frank...* As the prebasic (postnuptial) molt commences in early June, wood ducks spend hour after hour removing loose belly and breast feathers. Around loafing sites where such preening has taken place, the ground or water afterward is covered with these small feathers.

*Scott...* Ducks have a large preen (uropygeal) gland located at the base of the tail. The oil secreted by this gland is rich in fatty acids. Wood ducks use their bills to collect this oil and spread it on their feathers and legs. Without such lubrication, the feathers would lose their structure, dry out and weaken to the point where they would be useless for flight, insulation or water proofing. There is some evidence, too, that preen oil keeps the horny sheath of the bill from drying out and sloughing.

*Frank...* Studies have shown that preen oil may contain a precursor of vitamin D which can be synthesized by sunlight. There is speculation that, when absorbed through the skin of some birds or ingested during preening, the precursor may aid in the prevention of rickets.

*Scott...* Wood ducks can't reach their own head and some neck feathers with their bills, so will scratch these areas with their legs and feet. I have seen woodies stretch their necks and lay their heads upside down along their backs in order to lubricate their crests and head feathers.

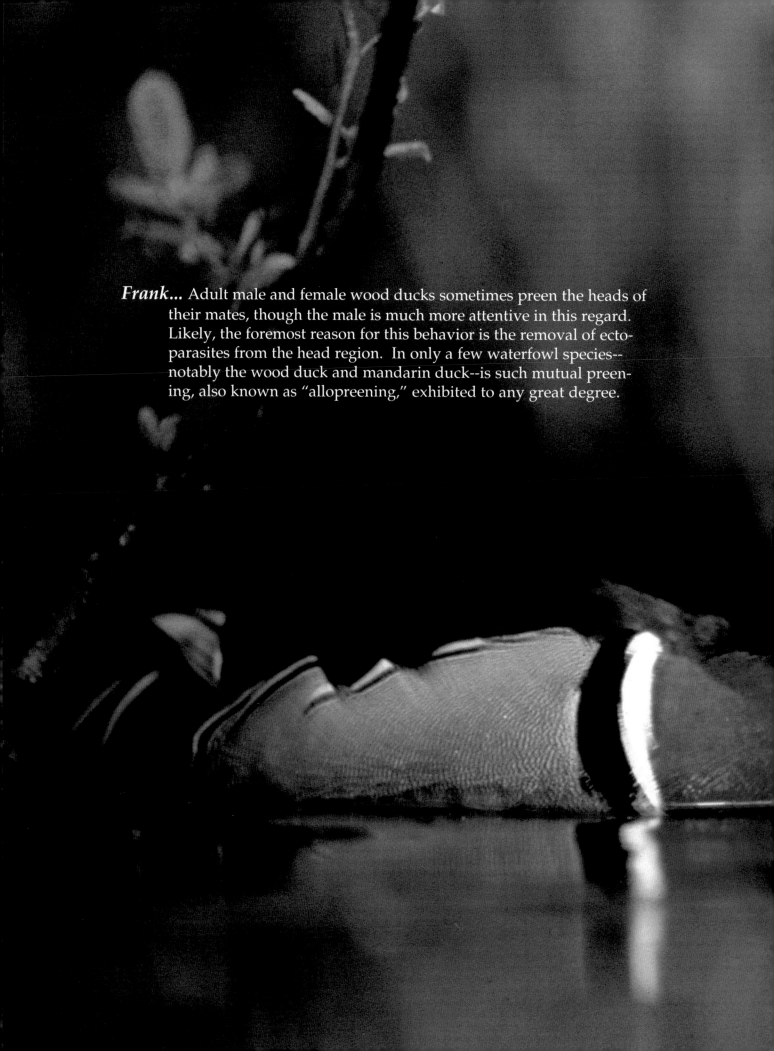

*Frank...* Adult male and female wood ducks sometimes preen the heads of their mates, though the male is much more attentive in this regard. Likely, the foremost reason for this behavior is the removal of ecto-parasites from the head region. In only a few waterfowl species--notably the wood duck and mandarin duck--is such mutual preen-ing, also known as "allopreening," exhibited to any great degree.

*Frank...* Courtship among adult wood ducks begins in August. Juveniles begin courtship in winter and spring. Some late-maturing hens probably do not initiate courtship until they return to their natal areas; some yearlings from very late broods may not breed.

Female woodies ultimately select their mates, but begin the whole mating process by giving up to seven "Coquette" calls--*ter-wee*--per minute to attract males.

Drakes--particularly those that have regained much of their definitive alternate (nuptial) plumage--respond with a number of types of calls given in concert with as

many as a dozen different ritualized body and plumage displays, most of which last less than a second. Among these calls are a burp (*fit*), basic call note (*jib*), whistle, preflight (*jii*) and hiss, and displays that include the "bill jab," "turning-the-back-of-the-head," "bill jerk," "preen-behind-the-wing," "chin-lifting," "display shakes" and "wing-and-tail-flashes."

A woodie hen also performs many of the displays, often to incite drakes to display for her. Similar to the behavior of males, a paired hen is quite likely to rush intruders. Depending on the circumstance, female use of this display may signal either sexual or aggressive intentions.

Displaying is evident throughout the lengthy courtship period in any wood duck population, but it is decidedly more prevalent in autumn and spring.

Early pairings in the autumn appear to be more temporary than are pair bonds established in late winter and spring. Nonetheless, a modest level of copulation occurs during autumn.

The pair bond is loose and temporary once the wood duck hen has chosen her mate, but it strengthens and deters intruders in the months and weeks preceding nesting. A paired hen is protected by her mate from harassment by other males while on wintering "grounds." On nesting grounds, the drake is constantly with or in close attendance to the hen through egg laying and for varying periods of incubation. A few drakes remain throughout the 30-day incubation period.

*Scott...* By the time wood ducks return to their breeding areas (usually the hens' birthplaces) in spring, most pairing is complete and competition among unmated males and conflict with mated males are not particularly common. Disputes that do occur usually are resolved by vocalizations and posturing.

Once a firm pair bond is established between a hen and drake wood duck, the hen usually leads the drake in their daily movements. Prior to then, however, during the courting phase, leading male mate candidates often strut their stuff in front of the prospective and discriminating hen. The drake will ride high in the water, its head and tail erect, to present itself large and impressive. His front position may be to monopolize the hen's view, shield her from the vision of other males or both.

*Frank...* Most courtship occurs on water in "bouts" lasting 1 to 20 minutes. It also involves acrobatic aerial flights of 2 to 20 drakes chasing a female for just several minutes at no more than 70 feet of altitude. These pursuits presumably test the fitness and tenacity of male suitors. Some drakes may drop out of the entourage before the hen lands with the remaining males to continue with the pageant. Pursuit flights are much less common in wood ducks than mallards and most other prairie ducks.

*Frank...* There is no evidence to suggest that wood ducks use plumage variations to distinguish among individuals of their own kind. Most likely, they identify each other primarily by vocalization. Sonograms indicate that variations in calls provide a means of individual recognition.

Male and female adult wood ducks have at least 12 distinct vocalizations (compared with 16 for the ring-necked pheasant, 28 for the wild turkey, and 14 or more for the mallard). Woodie ducklings have a known vocabulary of five calls.

*Scott...* Hen woodies are perhaps best known for a loud, plaintive, alarm (High-intensity Hauk) call they give when flushed off water. It is a distressing sound--*wee-e-e-ek! wee-e-e-ek*! I recall hearing it for the first time and thinking that the hen was seriously injured.

*Frank...* The hen's High-intensity Hauk call can be heard more than a quarter mile away--as far as, if not farther than, sound can be heard from any other duck species.

*Scott...* Wood duck drakes utter a variety of squeals and whistles. None is particularly loud or ear-catching. A person walking through the forest probably would dismiss the sounds as background noise.

*Frank...* Not uncommonly, one to three unmated drakes attach themselves to a mated pair. They tag along apparently with the intent of breeding with the female should the mated drake depart or falter in vigilance and the female accept his replacement. It seldom happens. Attachment of the mated male and spurious drakes may last through egg laying, but usually only the mated male accompanies the hen during incubation. Other males that approach within about 10 feet of the hen are certain to be warned off by sound, display or rush.

*Scott...* Unmated drakes that are regular associates of paired
wood ducks may be tolerated because they are easily
watched by the mated male so less of a worry, and they do
represent an extra set of senses to detect danger.

*Scott...* Allopreening has function in pair bonding. Aside from the hygienic purpose and value, it may serve as a test of the hen's submissiveness or readiness to be bred.

*Frank...* Unlike most prairie ducks (mallard, pintail, gadwall, wigeon, blue-winged teal and shoveler), wood ducks do not establish physical territories and do not show attachment to a particular place. Instead, wood duck breeding pairs exhibit willingness to move over an extensive area, adjusting their home range as floodwaters dictate. And unlike prairie ducks, woodies do not defend real estate. A mated wood duck male will attempt to protect his mate from the advances of other drakes. In essence, the hen becomes her mate's "moving territory." The mated male's defensive inclination begins to wane during the incubation period.

*Scott...* When the pair bond weakens during incubation and the mated drake lets down his guard a bit, unmated males are able to approach the mated hens more closely. The hens at this time usually are away from the nest to feed and rest. Sometimes--but certainly with less frequency than with mallards--the result of such flagging vigilance is a three-bird chase.

An unmated drake will suddenly rush at a mated pair from behind, occasionally grasping at the hen's tail with his bill. The pair will flush, with the lothario drake in hot pursuit. After a brief twisting flight, the unmated male breaks off the chase and the pair circles back to the approximate place where the episode began.

*Frank...* Not long ago, I saw an intruding woodie male harassing a mated pair. The female took flight with her mate following. They were followed in turn by the other male. The pair landed in the middle of the Mississippi River, a half mile away. Their antagonist landed nearby and swam toward the pair, both of whom promptly dove. They came up several yards away again and took flight. This time, the aggressive drake failed to follow them.

*Scott...* I once watched a three-bird chase that concluded with the hen landing in a tree. The unmated male landed alongside and attempted to mount her. The paired male then arrived and literally yanked the rogue drake off his mate.

*Frank...* When a wood duck pair bond is strongest, usually in the weeks prior to mating, both mates can be easily antagonized by the closeness, aggressiveness or posturing of other ducks, especially conspecifics (other wood ducks). Usually, when pairs confront each other, the first to take exception to the other's proximity will cause the other to retreat. This may first involve mutual threat displays and vocalizations by all four birds.

***Scott...*** Actual fights among wood ducks are rare. Such clashes usually amount to an intensive tight-circle chase of an interloper by a mated male. The latter snaps at the back, wing and tail feathers of the former and attempts to thrash his rival with his wings. After a few seconds, the interloper will break with the circling pattern and scutter away atop the water or fly off. Damage usually is no more serious than the contribution of a few scattered feathers to the fight arena. Although fights are brief, they are noisy and eruptive flurries. In one sense, they are counterproductive behavior for the wood duck, because they can attract predators to the area. Overall, however, these fights may be beneficial, because they may help to strengthen mates' pair bond.

*Frank...* Unmated hens appear on breeding and nesting grounds because their mates have been lost or have lost interest, or these hens are late-hatched birds of the previous year and are just reaching sexual maturity. Their Coquette calls can quickly draw as many as 20 males and incite the ritualized panoply of courtship calls and displays.

For reasons not clear, a paired female wood duck may be subject to attack by another male. If copulation occurs when the hen is unreceptive, the behavior is considered tantamount to "rape." Ornithologists use the term *forced copulation.*

Not infrequently, a mated drake must attempt to defend his hen against the aggressions of other males. The mated drake usually is successful, but not always. On occasion, the mate and an intruding drake may attempt to mount a hen at the same time.

A friend told me of an incident in which the attack of a hen by three woodie drakes was so vigorous and vicious that the hen was drowned.

*Scott...* Forced copulation is a noisy, seemingly violent scene, but it also is a way of maximizing a hen's productivity--an important factor in population recruitment. It can allow for second or third nesting attempts in the absence of a sexually vigorous mate or a new, time-consuming pair bonding.

*Frank...* A reliable source told me of seeing a nesting female woodie streaking toward her nest house on a direct line of flight. She literally flew through the entrance, with the male in close pursuit. The drake collided with the nest house and dropped dazed to the ground. It took 30 minutes for the male to recover sufficiently to walk to a water area. I'm sure that this was an unmated male intent on forced copulation.

***Scott...*** To give some perspective to the frequency of forced copulation, I have seen it hundreds of times with mallards, a few dozen times with lesser scaup (bluebills) and once with wood ducks.

*Frank...* Wood duck hens in the presence of unmated males likely are not at risk of forced copulation or intense harassment if they are not giving sexual signals (vocalizations or postures) to their mates or inciting the attention of prospective mates.

*Frank...* Wood ducks usually loaf in groups. Logs or "bars" where as many as 15 or more woodies congregate for loafing as breeding season wanes tend to be on the edge of water in an area sheltered from wind. They also tend to be fairly open, probably to give the birds' optimal viewing, maximum exposure to sunlight and a direct, unimpeded escape route.

A loafing log or bar becomes sort of a community gathering place, and is used again and again unless the loafers experience repeated disturbance there.

*Frank...* The amount of time that a wood duck has for resting, or "loafing," in its daily "budget" depends on the birds energy reserves and requirements. The more energy it has stored as lipids and lipid proteins, and the less it requires to maintain its vigor and reserves, the more time the woodie has to rest.

Seasonally, loafing takes place most often when foods are most available. Ambient air temperature also is a factor. Warm temperatures help grow desirable foods and draw less on the wood duck's energy reserves to maintain proper body temperature. In addition, this warm period of vegetation "green-up" is the time of maximum cover, so threats of predation are reduced.

*Scott...* Wood ducks loaf during part of every day--it is how they conserve energy in cold weather and warm. More than half of every day is devoted to loafing, usually from midmorning to late afternoon, when natural predators are relatively inactive and daytime temperatures are highest.

*Scott...* Loafing in groups allows individual wood
    ducks more freedom from constant alertness, in
    order to preen and catnap--more eyes are more
    vigilant.
        Even though woodies have a very wide
    field of vision, they are inclined to loaf either
    facing or looking in different directions. This,
    no doubt, is an antipredator "strategy."

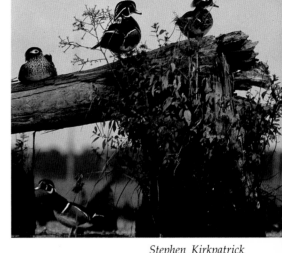

*Stephen Kirkpatrick*

*Frank...* Wood ducks are not usually disturbed by the
    closeness of other waterfowl species, nor are other
    ducks especially sensitive to woodies. In fact,
wood ducks often can be seen loafing alongside ducks of other species, such as
mallards, which likely are nesting or have nested in the area and seek the same quiet
loafing cover. After the breeding season, I have seen woodies and mallards loafing
together on logs and muskrat houses. Probably, they consistently loaf together until
premigratory flocks are formed in autumn.

*Scott...* Mated pairs of wood ducks may loaf apart from large groups or by themselves altogether to reduce sexual harassment of the hen by unmated males. Even when a pair is confident enough to join others at a loafing site, the drake remains watchful.

*Frank...* A wood duck pair will remain together continually from the time it is paired until the hen begins incubating her eggs. At the outset of incubation, the drake remains near the nest. Every morning and evening, the hen will leave the nest for an hour or two. She will fly to a familiar loafing site and call to the male. He will join her and serve as lookout while the hen feeds, bathes, preens and rests (copulation usually does not occur during incubation). The closer to egg laying, the stronger the pair bond.

*Scott...* Most wood duck pair bonds seem to weaken toward the end of the first week of incubation and definitely thereafter. While his mate stays with the eggs, the drake will increase his association with other males, often at loafing bars or logs. He will become increasingly less responsive to calls from the hen to join her, and eventually he will leave with other drakes to a place to molt.

*Frank...* Very few wood duck males "honor" the pair bond through the entire 30-day incubation period.

    If a hen woodie loses her clutch early in the incubation period of about 30 days (beginning after the last egg has been laid), she will mate again with her drake if he still is available, sexually vigorous and interested enough to protect her from the amorous aggressions of unmated males. If not, the hen will select another male with whom to mate and produce a second clutch.

*Scott...* Among wood ducks, there is quite a difference between sleeping and loafing. Most daytime resting involves catnaps and most sleeping occurs at night in roosts. But woodies sometimes will sleep during the day, such as after a lengthy or difficult migration flight or during prolonged and severe weather conditions.

*Scott...* I consider wood duck hens and drakes to be equally wary, but their relative wariness depends on the time of year. A hen is wariest when tending her brood. A drake is most wary when "escorting" his incubating mate when she loafs.

*Frank...* Daytime sleeping by wood ducks indicates their contentment, with minimal fear of danger, hunger sated, and no courtship or breeding demands. It occurs most frequently in midsummer when necessary activities are few and food resources and temperature most favorable. Most of their daytime sleeping occurs on logs, stumps, muskrat houses. And unlike many other ducks, woodies seldom sleep on the water. All ducks--indeed, most birds--sleep with bills or beaks tucked under their scapular feathers. This is logical in cold weather because the air is slightly warmed before inhalation. At such times of reduced alertness and particular vulnerability, the posture alters the bird's profile appearance, and so serves to foil immediate or easy recognition by predators.

Rarely do woodies sleep on the ice because rarely does ice occur where they reside.

*Frank...* To some extent, all waterfowl have some general roosting area where they can spend the night safe from disturbances and predators. Most seek the broad open waters of lakes, bays or sounds for this purpose. Wood ducks, however, reverse this procedure and fly to wetlands with dense overhead cover.

Many wood duck roosts are traditional and used year after year and throughout the year, but only by a few birds during the breeding season. Some roosts may be occupied by several thousand ducks from late summer to late winter.

Wood ducks will arrive at a roost site from about one-half hour before sunset until it is too dark to see, usually a half hour after sunset. They leave much more rapidly after daybreak and usually are gone within 30 minutes of sunrise.

Wood ducks tend to select roost sites in shallow-water areas with overhanging herbaceous or woody vegetation. The herbaceous vegetation includes plants such as duck potato, American lotus and bulrush, and wooded vegetation that includes buttonbush, willow and swamp privet. In utilizing dense overhead cover for roost sites, wood ducks reduce the risk of death from night-prowling barred owls and great horned owls.

**Frank...** By selecting riverine nesting habitats, wood ducks have reduced competition with other species of ducks. Riverine habitat is notorious for fluctuating water levels following precipitation, making ground nesting impractical. Wood ducks adapted by placing their nests in tree cavities created by time, weather, plant disease and other animals. Such adaptation avoided nest losses due to rising water and ground predators.

More than 90 percent of all wood ducks nest in natural cavities, most of which occur in mature and overmature trees, and smaller numbers in dead snags. Pileated woodpeckers and fox squirrels provide cavities that occasionally are used by wood ducks, but most cavities of sufficiently large size develop from heartwood decay, with wind breaking away a large branch or the top of the trunk to expose the interior of the cavity to the outside.

**Scott...** Although the pileated woodpecker is seen in all types of forest within its range, it shows strong preference for pockets of hardwoods near rivers and other aquatic areas. It is no accident, therefore, that the range of the pileated woodpecker coincides with that of the wood duck in the United States. The pileated also is North America's largest woodpecker and comparable in size to the adult wood duck. Hence, the nesting and roosting cavities it creates for itself are readily useable by woodies.

A pair of pileateds may "drill" only one new nest cavity and a few roost holes each year, but they also excavate hundreds of holes in dead or dying trees in search of grubs and other wood-boring insects, their major food during winter months. Most of these "grub holes" are too elongated for immediate use by wood ducks. Further decay, weathering and use by a progression of other birds may eventually make them attractive to woodies. Chickadees and tree swallows might be able to use a grub hole right away, followed by flickers and saw-whet or screech owls, and then by barred owls or wood ducks.

There is no doubt that, without pileated woodpeckers, we wouldn't have nearly the number of wood ducks that exist and thrive today.

*Frank...* There are two basic types of natural cavities used for nests by wood ducks. Most typical and favored is one that has a small entrance opening into a shaft 12 to 24 inches deep. Second is a shaft with a top opening--a so-called "bucket cavity."

Large trees approximately 18 to 36 inches in diameter and under some sort of environmental stress are most likely to produce suitable cavities. Woodies prefer small cavity entrances of about 10 to 12 square inches and cavity depths of 6 to 24 inches.

Cavities should be 8 to 14 inches in diameter to be of optimum value to wood ducks. Also, the higher the cavity on a tree, the more likely it will be used because high cavities are less likely to be detected by the primary nest predators--raccoons, squirrels and snakes. Since surviving wood duck hens return to nest where they were last successful, they are, therefore, most likely to use high cavities. Artificial "predator-proof" nest houses, of course, make lower heights more feasible.

Management for wood ducks--and for a wide variety of other forest wildlife--needs to stress saving mature trees and snags within a half mile of wetlands and streams, encouraging beaver ponds and farm ponds in wooded areas, and protecting the remnant bottomland hardwood swamps, particularly in the Mississippi Delta.

*Frederic Leopold*

*Frank...* In the late 1890s and the early 1900s, there was much concern by ornithologists that wood ducks would be exterminated by overhunting. At that time, hunting for waterfowl in most states lasted from September to April, and market hunting was prevalent. All this began to change in 1900, with the passage of the Lacey Act, which essentially outlawed commercial gunning. And in 1918, woodies were given protection from all hunting through enactment of the Migratory Bird Treaty Act with Canada. With complete protection that lasted until 1942, along with the emergence of scientific wildlife management, wood duck populations commenced to rebound.

Hunter bag limits in force from 1942 to present have prevented overharvest, enabling the wood duck to expand into marginal and former breeding habitat from which it had been extirpated. A steady increase in wood duck numbers has resulted in it being the second-most important species in duck hunters' bags in the Atlantic and Mississippi flyways. In a number of states--North and South Carolina, Georgia and West Virginia, for example--it has become number one.

Because of their secretive nature, wood ducks are impossible to census

visually. The one measure of their yearly status is obtained from hunters via band-recovery data. The proportion of the wood duck population harvested has remained about the same since at least 1955. Therefore, the numerical increase in harvest during this 35-year period reflects the proportion of increases in flywaywide populations.

Artificial "houses" for wood duck nesting are an adjunct to natural cavities. Because of the extensive nature of riverine habitats used by breeding wood ducks, natural cavities produce the vast majority of all young. The linear pattern of stream habitat makes it difficult to use nest houses effectively to increase production. Nevertheless and fortunately, where more concise wetlands occur--such as marshes, swamps, beaver and farm ponds--nest houses have contributed substantially to local wood duck populations.

Local "colonies" of breeding wood ducks build up where houses provide safe nest sites because successful, surviving hens return the following year to the same or a nearby nest site. A high proportion of surviving female young also return to their natal areas. (Only about 50 percent of adult wood duck hens survive from one year to the next.)

For nesting, houses that inhibit the entrance of arboreal predators usually are safer than most natural cavities. These houses produce more young, thereby building up local woodie populations to the point of saturating local habitats--at which time, overcrowding and competition for food resources limit further increase.

*Scott...* Paired wood duck hens begin to search for suitable cavities almost as soon as they reach their nesting areas. Most nest searching takes place between early morning to midmorning, after the woodie pair has eaten, bathed and preened. This is the quietest (therefore safest) time of the day, since most of the wood duck's major natural predators are sleeping. In sum, the pair is less likely then to be disturbed and their movements are less likely to draw unwanted attention to them or the vicinity.

That time also is when heat and light from the morning sun would be greatest for cavities and houses with east- and southeast-facing entrances.

It has been my experience that woodies readily select those nest sites over others with entries in different directions. Not all houses erected for wood duck nesting are used by woodies. It may take woodies awhile to locate them or to choose them over more familiar houses or cavities. And there may be something about the house position, exposure, height, etc., that is objectionable to woodies but not noticeable to us. Some houses may go unoccupied for several years; others may never be used.

It appears that a hen will do all the investigating of prospective natural cavities and artificial nest houses, while her mate follows along, anxiously watching her progress and watching intently for signs of danger. The drake often will keep up a low chattering call, much different than his usual repertoire of squealings. The chatter presumably is to reassure the hen of his presence and the absence of danger, particularly when she is inside a cavity. A different call or no call would seem to serve as an alert to the hen of something threatening.

Having flown to a cavity or nest house, the woodie hen will grasp the entry hole with her feet, with her wings outstretched for balance and to slow her momentum, and use her tail to brace her body against the tree or house (just as woodpeckers and other tree-climbing birds do). Her head and neck are thrust into the cavity, her wings folded and, assuming conditions of the cavity are acceptable, she will pivot forward on the entry "perch" and slide inside. By the timing of my motor-driven camera, I know this process from touch down to disappearance in the cavity can be little more than a full second. Once a hen is familiar with a cavity, her entries are entirely fluid and that rapid.

***Frank...*** The ideal entry to any wood duck nesting cavity is a horizontal ellipse, four inches wide and three inches high. Much smaller and woodie hens cannot fit through; much larger and such predators as adult raccoons can gain entry as well.

Within the wood ducks range, the hooded merganser is the only other species of waterfowl that seeks similar cavities. However, it is a diving duck, and its feeding habits place it at a disadvantage in competing with woodies for nesting sites in riparian habitat.

***Scott...*** The hooded merganser is an open water duck, so competition with woodies for nest sites seems to be most keen for cavities and houses immediately along the shoreline of lakes. I doubt that the competition is a serious limiting factor for either species.

On rare occasions, I see common mergansers "probing" wood duck nest houses. But this bird is not really a competitor because it mostly nests north of the woodies' range. In addition, it is too large to enter properly made entry holes to nest houses or the entrances of cavities that wood ducks would select.

*Frank...* A hen may choose the first cavity or house she investigates or she may investigate as many as five or six or more over the course of several days before selecting one. She also may revisit the same prospects a number of times before reaching conclusion. Proximity to the hen's birthplace, availability of suitable cavities and houses, and competition with other wood duck hens and starlings likely influence the choice.

Adults are more likely than younger woodies to select the same nest sites used the previous year. Yearlings frequently follow adults to the same nesting area and a familiar site, and sometimes deposit eggs in the adults' nests.

*Scott...* Inside a cavity, the wood duck hen may spend as much as half an hour examining its potentials or rounding out the base of dead wood or sawdust. Her mate waits impatiently outside. I have never seen a drake enter a nest cavity or house. Such entry is very rare.

Unless the cavity is unacceptable, the hen sometimes perches for several minutes in the entrance facing out. This may be for orientation or reacclimation to sunlight, but probably it is merely to determine what danger may be nearby.

When the hen decides to leave, the drake is close behind again. Quite often, the pair will fly a short distance to a perch or water within sight of the cavity. For a brief while, they scan the area to size up the location and locate additional cavities.

*Frank...* Although some wood ducks are known to nest as far as a mile from water, the closer to water the better when broods leave nest sites and travel overland to water. Houses placed over water on pipes or posts produce the best results.

*Scott...* Within a few days of nest site selection, a wood duck hen begins to lay eggs, usually at a rate of one a day. Sometimes a first egg is laid on the occasion of a hen's initial visit to the site. This probably occurs mostly (if not exclusively) with hens who were born or previously produced a successful clutch at that exact location.

Egg laying, like nest site searching, tends to occur in the morning.

*Frank...* Friend and waterfowl biologist Art Hawkins and I designed the first practical nest house in 1939. Our experiments were directed at providing alternative nesting sources for woodies since so much of the bottomland forests in central Illinois had been cleared, mostly for agricultural purposes. We also wanted to see if we could reduce wood duck nest predation, principally by raccoons and squirrels, and nest site competition with squirrels and starlings, and to determine if such artificial cavities could be produced in quantity at reasonable cost--assuming the ducks would use them.

Although our initial designs were less precise than those in use and recommended today, the houses were quickly occupied by nesting wood duck hens. Even so, it took more than 30 additional years to devise a nest house that was durable, inexpensive, weather-proof and predator-proof. Since then, other people have added refinements to the design.

*Frank...* Copulation reinforces the wood duck pair bond and supplies sperm for egg fertilization. It commences prior to egg laying and continues at intervals throughout the period of egg laying. There is no exact record of copulation frequency during this period, but it seems to be related in part to the viability of the male's sperm. A female wood duck may require several inseminations to fertilize her entire clutch.

*Scott...* According to my observations, mating by a wood duck pair occurs once or twice each morning and evening until the hen has laid the last egg of the clutch.

*Frank...* Before copulating, wood ducks typically isolate themselves from other ducks, especially other wood ducks that might interfere. So it is not surprising that their few precopulatory displays are relatively inconspicuous. These displays generally are not accompanied by auditory signals, but there is slight vocalization with the bill jerk.

     Males of many other duck species perform elaborate displays immediately prior to mating. In this regard, wood duck drakes' ritual precopulatory behavior can be hard to detect. The first real indication of intention to mate is signalled by the hen. She will assume a pronated (or "soliciting") posture on the water and sink until her back is nearly awash. Usually, but not always, and only if there are no disturbances, the male will climb onto the female from behind.

*Scott...* Inexperienced yearling drakes sometimes approach and attempt to mount from the side or front.

     When the drake first is on his mate, their combined weight submerges the hen. But the drake will grasp the hen's nape in his bill to aid in his balance and this, in turn, raises her head above the water.

     After copulation, the male releases the hen and quickly swims a short distance away and turns to face the hen with his crest erect. The entire process--from approach to swimming away--takes less than a minute.

*Frank...* If copulation is successful (and only about 20 percent of attempts are), both the male and female wood ducks will perform postcopulatory displays that apparently function to reaffirm their pair identity.

*Scott...* Invariably after mating, a woodie male, and especially the female, will fan their wings to dry them. This also is considered to be one of the postcopulatory displays.

     On several occasions, I have seen wood duck hens that had the white facial markings of a drake. Both were courted by drakes and were paired, and at least one nested successfully. I have not been able to determine if this anomaly was hormonally or genetically linked.

*Frank...* When using natural cavities, hen wood ducks cover their initial eggs with woody material from the sides of the cavity, or leaves or grasses brought in previously by other animals. Neither hens nor drakes transport foreign matter to fashion a nest. The principle covering material is breast down, and this is added in earnest by the hen after she lays her fourth egg. She plucks her own down, eventually forming a plumage depression, or "brood patch," on her chest.

Wood duck eggs are dull white, but sometimes stained brown from moist, decayed matter in the cavity. They each weigh about one and a half ounces. The average woodie clutch size is 12. And of clutches neither abandoned nor somehow destroyed, 10 or 11 of those eggs will hatch on average.

In areas where there is a high density of nesting wood ducks and nest houses are closely spaced, we can expect to see "dump nesting." This occurs when one hen deposits her eggs in a nest being used by another hen. As many as 40 or more eggs have been found in a single nest. Except for the very large clutches (which simply can't be well-incubated), a fairly high percentage of the nest composite will hatch--assuming the nest isn't abandoned or destroyed. There is very little difference between nest success of normal and dump nests.

Sometimes two hens (usually an adult and yearling) will both attempt to nest in the same house or cavity. Occasionally, such intrusion leads to strife, with one of the birds injured or killed by the other.

*Scott...* Wood duck hens don't get very serious about incubating until the last egg is laid. Some incubating is done prior to then, but most insulation of the growing clutch is loose feather down. Since eggs are laid at a rate of one a day, immediate incubation would result in the ducklings hatched on different days. By "withholding" incubation, the hen essentially schedules a fairly simultaneous hatch.

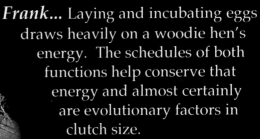

**Frank...** Laying and incubating eggs draws heavily on a woodie hen's energy. The schedules of both functions help conserve that energy and almost certainly are evolutionary factors in clutch size.

Incubation of wood duck eggs takes place over about 30 days, depending on clutch size, weather and hen disposition. Some woodie hens simply are impatient with the process or lack the full maternal instinct.

**Scott...** During the incubation period, the hen leaves the nest twice a day--usually in early morning and again in mid- to late afternoon--to feed, rest, bathe and preen, generally in the company of her mate, at least until his interest wanes.

*Stephen Kirkpatrick*

*Frederic Leopold*

*Frank...* About two days before hatching takes place, small cracks start to appear near one end--the blunt end--of each viable wood duck egg. Soon thereafter, the fully developed embryos begin to cheep intermittently and scrape against the inner wall of the shell. Eventually, the hatchling uses its egg tooth--a sharp, horny deposit on the tip of the bill--to cut a hole in the shell from the inside. This extraction, or "pipping," takes an hour or two.

   For the first few hours after hatching, woodie ducklings are soggy and almost lifeless. When finally dry, they are very rambunctious and vocal, and the hen's weeks of solitude on the nest are decidedly at an end.

   A woodie hen actually begins to communicate with her young when the latter are still inside their eggs. She uses a soft "Maternal call"--*kuck, kuck, kuck*--at a rate of about one note per five seconds.

*Jack Dermid*

David McEwen

Ray Cunningham

Jack Dermid

*Frank...* A hen's rapid calling incites her young to a frenzy of jumping, bumping and peeping--like so many furry, noisy ping-pong balls in a lottery wheel. The ducklings vie to clamber up to the cavity opening, by leaping, using their sharp decurved toe claws and flapping their undeveloped wings.

Mostly one at a time, the ducklings reach the entrance, pause momentarily, peep loudly, then jump, with wings oscillating and tail feathers outspread. The hen swims or walks nervously about, continuing to incite the laggards. If danger appears, she will switch to a Hauk warning call that "freezes" the ducklings still in the nest. When the danger passes, they are "released" by resumption of the Maternal call.

Frederic Leopold

*Scott...* Quite often, when it is time for the ducklings to leave the nest--about 24 hours after hatching--the hen will first spend several minutes perched at the cavity or house entrance, facing out and surveying for danger. If everything appears all right, she will adjourn to a nearby branch or on the ground or in water below and commence to call at an accelerated rate of three to four notes per second.

Woodie ducklings that leave cavities or houses over water have a considerably safer and less rude introduction to terra firma. I have seen ducklings plummet 50 feet to ground without receiving injury. I also watched one duckling jump from more than 25 feet to a cement sidewalk. It bounced like a sodden tennisball and, showing no sign of damage, scurried to join its mother and siblings.

Nest exodus takes only about five minutes and almost always occurs before midmorning. A hen may spend an hour or more calling to ducklings still at the nest but unable to leave. Eventually, she will depart to water or cover, with her brood following in a compact cluster. A hen also will leave if she suspects danger nearby and even if ducklings are calling in the nest.

Some noted early ornithologists, including Alexander Wilson and John James Audubon, wrote that wood ducks use their bills to carry ducklings from nests. Such behavior has not since been credibly reported.

*Frederic Leopold*

David McEwen

*Frank...* Most of what we know about predation on wood ducks concerns nest mortality. Predation appears to be the cause of destruction of about 48 percent of wood duck nests in natural cavities. Another 12 percent of woodie nests are simply deserted, and predation undoubtedly is an influence in many of these cases.

The major predator of wood duck nests north of the Mason-Dixon line is the raccoon. In the South, rat snakes do the most damage. Other significant nest (egg) predators are gray and fox squirrels, flickers and red-bellied woodpeckers. Starlings also damage eggs but pose more of a problem by competing for use of cavities or "parasitizing" nests (adding their own eggs to a wood duck clutch).

*Frederic Leopold*

*Scott...* From the standpoint of human sensitivities, predation on wood ducks--or on any wildlife species, for that matter--may seem to be cruel and senseless. But predation is integral to the natural rhythms of our organic universe. Just as the woodie sometimes preys on insects for food, some other animals occasionally prey on woodies. Such killing is a necessary part of the continuum and balance of life.

To some extent, predation has fashioned the wood duck. For many millennia, predators have taken young, weak and unwary woodies. Predation has influenced wood duck numbers to some degree and it certainly has influenced the species' behavior and habitat selection. That the woodie is among the wariest of ducks, if not the wariest, that it survives in predator-laden habitat, that it nests in cavities off the ground, that its colorful plumage is camouflaged by white markings, that not all members of the species molt at the same time, that woodies are gregarious, that their preferred habitat is sheltered riparian areas, etc., etc., are by no means coincidence. They are adaptations to survival--principally survival from predation.

*Jack Dermid* (previous pages)

*Frank...*Less is known of predation on woodie ducklings. Some of the predators of woodie ducklings are hawks (especially the red-shouldered [immature female goshawk on following page]), owls (especially barred and great-horned), fish (especially largemouth bass, bowfin and pickerel), bullfrogs, snapping turtles, snakes, alligators, mink and even great blue herons. Somewhat less than half of ducklings that hatch survive to fledging (flight), a period of about two and a half months.

Because their habitat subjects them to many and diverse predators, wood ducks experience higher brood loss than does any other waterfowl species.

Little is known of predation on adult wood ducks, except that raccoons kill an appreciable number of incubating hens. I have witnessed a peregrine falcon attack a wood duck and have seen remnants of adult woodies left by great horned owls and mink. Alligators undoubtedly take a fair number of woodies in southern swamplands.

Human hunting removes approximately 20 to 25 percent of the autumn wood duck population. Natural mortality, including disease, accidents and predation, accounts for the balance of all losses that amounts to about 50 percent of the woodie population annually. Breeding wood ducks have successfully raised slightly more young in recent decades than the number of birds lost by the total woodie population. This accounts for the slow but steady increase in wood ducks at least since the 1960s.

*Frank...* Since there are more drakes than hens in the wood duck breeding population, un-paired males tend to consort during the breeding season. They stay in close proximity to mated pairs, awaiting opportunity to breed with unattended hens or abandoned hens with unsuccessful broods.

*Scott...* At some point during the incubation period, drake wood ducks discontinue association with their mates. These males then begin to congregate near feeding areas with other "deserters" and with the same unmated drakes they worked hard to keep away from their hens a few weeks earlier. Within a few weeks, such congregations can number a dozen or more.

Just before ducklings are urged from their nest cavities to spend several critically formative months in their mothers' charge, the drakes depart, often en masse, to find suitable areas to begin the annual molt.

The larger the group of wood ducks, the more difficulty I have getting photos of them. In large groups, they tend to position themselves to face in different directions. Whether this is a predator defense, a factor of social hierarchy or both, I'm not sure. In any case, the woodie drake in such circumstance is intensely vigilant.

*Frank...* The gregarious nature of wood ducks also appears to be an adaptation to predation in habitats where its enemies are numerous and close-by. Danger detected by one bird in a group is quickly conveyed to the others by erect posture, vocalization or sudden flight.

Wood ducks tend to hide under protective overhead vegetation a large part of the time, much more so than other duck species. And I have found that, when they have been feeding with mallards and other species, woodies are the first to detect my presence-- through sound and movement--and flee.

*Scott...* I don't consider wood ducks to be particularly secretive, but they definitely are wary. Many people consider the black duck to be the wariest species, but I find them no more alert and cautious than the mallard, and the woodie is at least as easily spooked.

*Frank...* While feeding, swimming or resting, the woodie unquestionably is the wariest of ducks. But in flight, as singles, pairs or larger flocks, it is less wary than many other species. Wood ducks tend to decoy with little encouragement and without careful inspection.

**Scott...** Regardless of how well a bird preens and otherwise maintains its plumage, the feathers do wear out and are replaced each summer by a process known as molting. A wood duck's feathers become especially worn from its dodging flight through brush and forest. The hen's frequent entry and departure from the narrow opening of a nest cavity tends to wear her back feathers.

**Frank...** Drake woodies are the first ducks to begin the annual prebasic (postnuptial) molt. This leads to the basic (eclipse) plumage, with which the drakes resemble hens.

    The first males to begin the molt start by losing their bronze side feathers. The rest of their brilliant plumage is lost in about a month, then they lose all their flight feathers. The flight feathers are replaced after three or four weeks. Thereafter, the alternate (nuptial) begins to replace the drab basic plumage over the course of six to eight weeks.

**Scott...** Molting in summer months is highly advantageous.  At this warmest time of the year, foods and daylight are at their peaks.  Woodies can channel most nutrient intake into feather development and less energy is required to maintain body temperature.  Vegetation is most lush during this season, providing maximum shelter, especially necessary during the flightless period of about one month.

**Frank...** All drake woodies do not molt at the same time.  Some can begin to molt four to six weeks later than those that started earliest.  The early molters are in full breeding regalia in early September.

Nonbreeding wood duck hens and those that lose their nests and do not renest molt on about the same schedule as that of drakes.  Brood-rearing delays most hens by six to eight weeks in undergoing the prebasic molt.

Clearly, timing of molt is determined partly by the chronology of nesting.  The first hens to nest (and their mates) are the first to molt.

**Scott...** Wood duck drakes that mate and molt earliest have an advantage over late nesters and yearlings.  By the time the latter males have grown the bright nuptial plumage, sometimes not before late October, the early birds have had a significant head start in courting prospective mates.

**Frank...** I have counted the feathers on an adult drake wood duck.  The numbers were 4,486 on the head, 2,634 on the body and 536 on the wings, for a total of 7,656.  Their combined feather weight was 1.25 ounces.

*Scott...* Once a wood duck hen gathers her brood, I am seeing her and her progeny for the last time. And I have no idea where they go, but it most assuredly is some remote back-water, away from the sights, sounds and intrusions of my summer neighborhood.

*Frederic Leopold*

*Frank...* With her brood in tow, a wood duck immediately moves to water. It may involve overland treks of a mile or more. Once there and refreshed, the troupe then heads for a densely vegetated wetland. Such a place may require a journey of several days to a week, at a casual swimming pace of about a mile per day.

      For the first week, the brood stays close together and near or under concealing cover. The hen/brood bond is very tight during the ducklings first several weeks. And even though a hen may attend her brood for one to two months, the bond begins to diminish after three to five weeks. It usually is the ducklings that become independent, rather than the hen.

*Stephen Kirkpatrick (next facing pages)*

*Scott...* Of all the waterfowl I've observed, a hen wood duck with a brood is the wariest.

*Frank...* A wood duck hen is very protective of her brooding young. Even so, on average, only 25 to 50 percent of the ducklings that leave the nest survive to flight stage at 60 to 70 days of age. The wood duck experiences greater brood loss than does any other common duck species. Extant broods decline from 10 to 11 ducklings at nest departure to about 5 at flight age, but entire broods sometimes are lost. Age ratios indicate that the average adult hen raises 2.9 young to flight. Of course, this also includes females that were *unsuccessful* nesters. It appears that 20 to 30 percent of hens may lose their entire broods.

*Scott...* It's easy to look at the increase in wood duck populations during the past 60 years and be a bit complacent about the species' future, just as ornithologists were about passenger pigeons when billions flocked our continent 150 years ago, and just as lumbermen were when confronted with seemingly inexhaustible stands of trees before the turn of the century.

Nevertheless, there are promising signs for the wood duck. Waterfowling certainly is much better managed than it was a century ago; the wooded riverine habitats that woodies seek out are less susceptible to drought than the prairie pothole areas that so many of our other duck species use; and while logging is still done, it's now common practice to leave a forested buffer area of a few hundred feet along any rivers or other bodies of water. Two fairly well separated wood duck populations--one east of the Mississippi and another in the Pacific Northwest--help assure that natural disasters won't decimate the species. Wood ducks are among the most popular, prolific of species kept by aviculturists and zoos.

Balancing things is the relatively southern nesting range of the wood duck. Many of its nesting areas correspond to places of large human population growth, and people find watery areas just as attractive for habitation as do wood ducks. Species such as the bufflehead, goldeneye and common merganser that nest farther north are at an advantage here. Environmentalists predict that global warming may radically change the habitats to which the wood duck has adapted.

*David McEwen*

Change is inevitable. The question is how fast things will change and how quickly the wood duck (along with all other life) can continue to adjust. I don't have the answers. But wishful thinking and knowledge of the species' resilience lead me to believe that the wood duck's future is indeed promising.

If there's one thing you take away from this book, I hope it's an awareness of just how special the wood duck is and how it helps make our world the beautiful place it is.

*David McEwen*

*Frank...* Food, more than any other factor, regulates the abundance and well-being of natural populations. Due to the wood duck's proven ability to use, locate and exploit new sources of food, I am confident that the species can continue to adapt to altered habitats in the years ahead.

Because people in North America are becoming increasingly aware of the multiple values of wild or at least untamed places, and because there seems to be growing public awareness that human impositions on the environment are no longer self-correcting, I am convinced that our own future generations will have greater sensitivity to and appreciation for the landscape and its wildlife. It may be wishful thinking, but I really believe that wood ducks and other valued wildlife have excellent prospect because society in general no longer takes for granted our continent's environmental well-being and productivity.

Wildlife scientists now know how to manage effectively for healthy wood duck populations. But management is a dynamic process. And like wood ducks, management requires the right types and amounts of "food"--manpower, opportunity, authority, equipment and insight. For wildlife science and management to keep apace of changing landscapes and changing human expectations for wildlife, they must have those resources. About this, I am at least hopeful.

Despite--or perhaps in spite of--my general optimism about the future of woodies, I have a lingering concern. Even if the trend of heightened public interest and appreciation for the natural environment continues, and even if wildlife science is allowed the wherewithal to maintain its momentum, there is a potential pitfall. As well-intentioned as society may be about its natural heritage, it cannot continue to tolerate its own rates of growth and sprawl. All bets are off if humankind's numbers and byproducts broach the tolerance levels of ecological sustainability.

Most wildlife--and wood ducks in particular--are remarkably adaptable. But there are limits. For the good of wood ducks, for ourselves, for all things, we must not press those limits.

For me, wood duck populations are, in a sense, symbolic of human treatment of the natural world. Their resurgence within the past century has paralleled, in time and place, our society's efforts to recover from and protect against the ecological abuses of times past. I believe, too, that woodies also may serve the future in a small way as a bellwether of a much larger arena of environmental responsibility.

*Stephen Kirkpatrick*          *David McEwen* (next facing pages)

# FIELD NOTES...

# FIELD NOTES...